BAKE LIKE A PRO!

BAKE LIKE A PRO!

Falynn Koch

:01

First Second
New York

Baking delicious desserts is fun,
but injuries are not!

Ask an adult to help you when recipes
require handling knives and or using the oven.
Be sure to use pot holders when handling hot items.

Always wash your hands before handling
food and never eat uncooked dough or batter.
Trust me, food-borne illness is not fun!

Messy kitchens are hazardous!
Clean up spills on the floor and put sharp or
hot items in safe places when not in use.

Every kitchen should be equipped with a
fire extinguisher and smoke alarm.
Make sure they are in working order!

2

Sage, turn them into a meal, only using heat.

No problem, *easy!*

Yeah! Let's get cookin'!

Aestus cibus!

AHH!

FOOSH

Uuugh...

Not bad!

Now they're edible. What's the big deal?

SSSS

SSSS

The **big deal** is that baking is about more than being **edible**.

VMPH

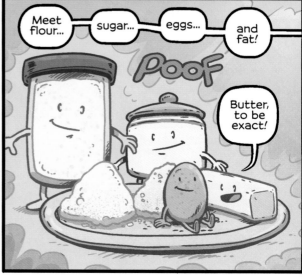

Meet flour...

sugar...

eggs...

and fat!

POOF

Butter, to be exact!

Now listen up!

I wanna get outta here and go see my friends!

So, let's get to work!

Pound cake, huh? *Looks easy.* Flour, butter, sugar, eggs, milk, salt, baking powder, vanilla extract... Yep, everyone's here.

vmm

Flour! You're up first!

Okaaay...

What are you doing?!

You're not going to *sift* me?

Scooping, I need two cups.

I don't know what sifting is.

WHAT?

Sifting is an important part of working with flour!

GAH!

Z Z Z

When flour sits unused, air escapes. The flour compacts.

Sifting puts the air back in...

WUMP

between all the tiny pieces of milled flour!

Compacted flour and sifted flour take up a *different* amount of space! Even when using the **same** cup!

Whatever.

No, no, no—

PMPF

EEK

NOO!

11

15

18

20

Let's also talk about measuring dry ingredients correctly. Sugar, could you explain?

Measuring cups and measuring spoons measure by volume, so they must be filled completely.

Overfill the cup or spoon with dry ingredients, like flour, salt, baking powder, and white sugar.

Then level it off with something flat, pushing the excess back into the container.

Flour should be sifted first **before** being measured like this.

Yeah, flour already told me about sifting.

Mm-hmm, I did indeed.

A traditional sifter looks like a can with a handle, a crank that turns, and a screen. This aerates the flour as it moves through.

But not everyone has a sifter, so you can also use a mesh strainer, called a sieve, or we can mimic it by using a whisk.

Omph!

Gently whisk us together. This will add air, so it's fluffier.

This isn't real sifting...

But it's better than scooping straight into compressed flour and will make your flour measurement more uniform every time.

When you add other dry ingredients to flour, like **me**, salt, or baking soda, sift us together too!

Then we are mixed together evenly!

Another important thing that many recipes don't stress is the temperature of butter.

The difference in temperatures can completely change its use.

POP POP POP POP POP

Frozen butter is used for doughs to keep them cold and hold their shape.

Cold butter is perfect for rolling between layers of dough, like filo pastry.

Room temperature butter that still holds its shape is ideal for creaming.

Warm butter that's been left out too long will spread a lot when baked.

Some recipes want melted butter, but it shouldn't be *hot!*

POKE

-32°F

40°F

65°F

80°F

+95°F

Why don't recipes explain these things?

It seems important!

Many *cookbooks* do bring up ingredient temperature...

but an **individual** recipe may not.

27

Recipes used to be passed down from one family member to another or from master to apprentice.

People learned by *example*.

Bakers learned *how* different baking methods worked...

without knowing exactly *why* they did.

Understanding the science of baking improves the skills of both the expert and the amateur baker especially since recipes don't always explain every word or technique.

I'll never remember all this.

It's best to learn by doing it.

Whaddya say we make some cookies?

Chocolate chip?

CHOCOLATE CHIP COOKIES

I'll find the recipe!

No need!

Got one right here!

It's a classic!

On the chocolate chip bag?

Tell me, what ingredients do we need?

We already have butter, sugar, eggs, flour, vanilla, and salt.

Chocolate chips are needed.

Also brown sugar and baking **soda**.

Milk and baking **powder** can sit this one out.

1 cup (2 sticks) butter

1/2 cup white sugar

2 cups flour

1 tsp vanilla extract

2 large eggs

1 bag chocolate chips

3/4 tsp salt

1 cup packed brown sugar

1 tsp baking soda

Always have the standards—like bowls, measuring cups, spoons, and spatulas—out.

But what special tools are needed?

We also need cookie sheets, and if available, a stand mixer and cooling rack.

The fluffy beaten-up butter holds on to that air.

Adding it to the finished dough or batter.

Hello!

When baked, the trapped air expands from heat, making the dough grow and rise.

OH!

The Creaming Method is one of **five** methods of controlling the amount of air and rise in a baked good. We will discuss them in detail as we try them all out.

Creaming Method

Muffin Method

Biscuit Method

Dough Method

Egg Foam Method

Now that we know what **this** method does and how to do it, let's finish this cookie dough!

After creaming, add the brown sugar and vanilla.*

*After each step, combine new ingredients using the paddle at medium speed.

Add the eggs, incorporating them one at a time.

Add the sifted dry ingredients, pouring them in slowly and gently.

No need to wait for all the dry ingredients to be mixed in. Add us now!

It's our little dough babies!

Aww!

Bake up big and strong! But not **too** strong!

A lot of factors go into making the perfect cookie. This recipe wouldn't have turned out so well if we were baking at a high altitude.

What happens at high altitude?

The air pressure is lower, which affects baking.

Eat me next!

No, *me!*

Air pressure is the weight of the atmosphere pressing down on objects. Recipes are typically written for pressure at sea level.

O_2

N

Air Molecules

CO_2

H

HURG!

At a high altitude, like in the mountains, there's less pressure, which can cause several issues.

HA!

hmph!

Foods take longer to cook. The temperature and bake times need to be increased.

I'm so dry!

Liquids evaporate faster. Flour and liquid amounts need to be changed so the batter isn't gummy or dry.

Whoa there!

Gases expand more, doughs rise faster, and baking soda or powder should be decreased.

37

Less flour makes thin and crispy cookies.

Thick cookies have **more** flour and spread less.

For soft cookies, use **cake flour,** with less protein.

Different amounts of flour, the type of flour, and the gluten formed affects the texture of a cookie.

Chewy cookies can use **bread flour,** with more protein.

Oh!

Overmixing dough creates tight gluten and smooth cookies.

Less mixing keeps gluten loose, making craggy cookies.

So gluten needs **water** to uncoil and **agitation** to bond.

But there wasn't any water in the chocolate chip cookie recipe.

Every recipe has water in it, but it might be **hidden** in other ingredients.

45

Egg **whites** provide **strength**.

And **yolks** hold the **flavor**.

Exactly!

If a recipe asks for **whole** eggs, **only** egg whites, or **only** egg yolks, it's asking for a **reason**.

This affects cookies in a few ways.

Using only whites will mean more rise and very fluffy but dry cookies.

Using only yolks will mean less rise and dense, cake-like cookies.

Whole eggs create your average cookie texture, using the best of both.

What happens without any egg at all?

All baked goods need some kind of binder.

Flour can bind, but eggs help without using any gluten.

Flour and eggs work together!

Then, eggs and flour are the most important ingredients in baking!

They certainly are **not!**

Hmph!

Like me, shortening! I'm solid at room temperature, don't contain water, and don't melt as fast as butter!

THHBT

Shortening: 100% vegetable fat

My dairy proteins provide the distinct **buttery** flavor *and* brown when cooking.

mmhm

Butter: 80% animal fat 15% water 5% protein

Using **me** will make baked goods softer *but dense.* With no water in me, I don't steam when baked.

That's **great** for cutout cookies and intricate piecrusts.

Not for things you want to expand!

SMMUSH

See? That does mean I'm better!

BUMP

OH!

I never said that, you *dairy dummy!*

HMPH!

SHOVE

We'll see who is **best!**

Hey! Hands off the fat!

THHBBT

49

Leavening is anything that creates bubbles, helping the dough to rise. Baking **soda** and its cousin baking **powder** create air bubbles, or gases, chemically.

Cousin!

POP

There are **four** ways to leaven. Baked goods need **at least** one or a combination.

Air trapped by creamed **butter** or whipped **eggs**.

Evaporated water trapped in **butter** and **eggs**.

Chemical leavening making carbon dioxide bubbles.

CHOMP

CHEW

Yeast organisms that create carbon dioxide as waste.

Baking **soda** is the common name of **sodium bicarbonate**.

I react when combined with liquid **acid**.

Acid is the molecule that gives some food their **sharp** or **sour** tastes.

The more acidic it is, the stronger the reaction baking soda will have with it.

The reaction creates a fizzy *explosion* of carbon dioxide bubbles!

Whee!

PSSSSSST

When I am mixed with potassium bitartrate, also called cream of tartar, it makes baking powder!

Because of cream of tartar, I make carbon dioxide with **any** liquid.

Even plain water.

In 1791, Nicolas Leblanc invented baking soda. But back then, **before** home fridges existed, activating me was difficult. Many of the mild, tasty, acidic ingredients best for baking didn't keep long.

Is this sour cream or *sour* sour cream?

Before that, creaming and egg foams leavened baked goods but had to be done by hand, without any machines.

More cake*!*

And **way before** that, yeast was the go-to leavener, but it can be tricky to use and takes a long time to rise.

Rise already!

What's wrong with you?

In 1843, Alfred Bird created easy-to-use baking powder by adding cream of tartar.

Here! Now you don't have to use that old *sour* sour cream anymore!

Great! I'll finally throw it out after fifty-two years!

We are so easy to use, a whole new baking method was created: the **Muffin Method.**

And methods that never used us **before** often include us **now** as a backup.

Although we're similar, be sure not to substitute one of us for the other.

Using only soda, you'll get less rise, more spread, and a craggy texture.

Using only **powder** will give more rise and a smaller diameter.

With drop cookies, you can adjust your leavening to achieve texture preference.

When cutout cookies have leavening...

FISSSSSSSSS

—HEY!

AHHH

POOF!

Depending on the method used, many baked goods are in the quick bread category, even though they are not foods we typically consider to be *bread*. Take me, **the waffle**, made using the Muffin Method.

You can use the **Muffin** Method to make **bread**, which might be **waffles?**

Yep!

CRUNCH

Don't let the names confuse you!

Is cake *bread?*

What about pan*cakes?*

No.

Yes.

Hold on, that seems **intentionally** confusing.

I mean, who really cares?

Who cares if **bread** is **cake** or if **cake** is **bread** if they can be so similar?

Baking wizards care! That's who!

I don't want to eat **bready** cake or **cakey** bread.

Knowing the methods lets **you** control the outcome.

Some terms in baking may overlap or create *similar* baked goods, **but** the most important thing is the method.

Here are the basics for the Muffin Method explained.

Combine all your **dry** ingredients together.

Combine all your **wet** ingredients, separately.

Then mix dry and wet **together** and bake.

That's all.

Um, this is really *wet* and **lumpy.**

That's okay. This method creates **batter,** not *dough.* **And—** you **want** it lumpy, *not* smooth.

It's a good look for me, don't ya think?

CORN BREAD

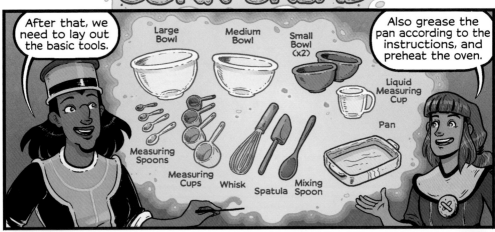

After that, we need to lay out the basic tools.

Also grease the pan according to the instructions, and preheat the oven.

Large Bowl
Medium Bowl
Small Bowl (x2)
Liquid Measuring Cup
Pan
Measuring Spoons
Measuring Cups
Whisk
Spatula
Mixing Spoon

Dry ingredients are organized and whisked together.

This recipe has cornmeal flour *and* wheat flour, but you can make it using **only** cornmeal if you like.

All-cornmeal corn bread will be gluten-free and a little crumbly.

With some wheat flour added, it will be fluffier.

Salt
1 tsp

Baking Soda
1/2 tsp

Baking Powder
1 TBSP

Cornmeal
2 cups

Flour
1 cup

Large Bowl

Wet ingredients are mixed together.

With the eggs cracked and beaten separately before being added.

Eggs

Whole Milk

Butter-milk?

Buttermilk

As in, **buttery** milk?

OH!

White Sugar
1/4 cup

Butter 1 stick (melted)

3 (whole)

1/2 cup

1 1/2 cup

Medium Bowl

Wait!

GLUG!

Ugh! You're sour!

I *prefer* the word tangy!

What a cruel trick of a name!

Buttermilk is the liquid left after churning butter. It has a strong acidity and will activate baking soda.

If you say so.

Now join the rest of the wet ingredients.

Stop mixing as soon as the dry ingredients are moist.

Then pour the batter into the pan right away, lumps and all.

63

BANANA BREAD

Banana bread's sweetness and flavor is mostly from **overripe** banana. So make sure they are older and soft!

Organizing for this bread is almost the same as the corn bread.

Grease the pan.

Turn on the oven.

350°F

Get out the tools.

Large Bowl
Small Bowl
Measuring Cups
Wire Cooling Rack
Stand Mixer (if available)

Medium Bowl
Measuring Spoons
Whisk
Spatula
Mixing Spoon
Paddle Attachment

Combine and sift dry ingredients.

Flour 1 1/2 cups
Baking Soda 1 tsp
Salt 1 tsp

Combine all the wet ingredients.

I need to be smashed up, so my natural sugar is distributed evenly!

Brown Sugar
Butter 1 stick
Very Ripe Banana
Eggs 2 (whole)
Sour Cream 1/3 cup

(packed) 2/3 cup
(room temperature)
(2 to 4) 1 1/2 cups
(cracked and whisked)
Chopped Walnuts 1/2 cup (optional)

66

Yeast is **alive**, right? How does that work?

Um, Sage...

...**everything** is alive in this kitchen.

I mean in a *normal* kitchen!

Ha ha, **yes**, yeast is alive all on its own, without any magic.

My scientific name is *Saccharomyces cerevisiae*, or "sugar-eating fungus."

I can leaven bread, but my cousins also ferment beverages, ripen cheeses, and produce antibiotics.

POP

I eat sugar for energy, so I can multiply and make more yeast!

I'll eat all kinds of sugar!

When I eat sugar I also create **two** by-products!

Sucrose is granulated sugar.

Fructose or glucose is honey or fruit sugars.

Maltose is the sugar in flour starch.

TOOT

Ethanol alcohol

and

carbon dioxide!

The carbon dioxide creates tiny pockets of gas inside of dough.

The ethanol alcohol liquid provides yeasty flavor but steams away when baked.

TOOT
TOOT

To make bread rise, you have to take care of me!

I'm like a strange little pet!

Too **much** sugar creates too much yeast.

And I will **drown** in my own alcohol.

Too **little** sugar, and there will be too little yeast.

And I won't make enough gas to raise the dough.

If I'm too **cold**, I'll eat sugar very slowly...

or not at all.

um...

POKE POKE

ZZZZZ

If I'm too **hot**, I'll die!

And I can't be revived.

This happens from 130°F to 140°F or higher

PIZZA DOUGH

Do we mix dry yeast into the other *dry* ingredients like flour and salt?

If we were using **instant** yeast, we would.

But we're using **active** yeast. It has to be added to warm water.

It will need about ten minutes to *"bloom,"* or activate.

No warmer than 120°F! Remember, I'll die if I'm too hot!

I'll bloom with only water, but adding sugar gives me some food to eat right away.

As the yeast is waking up, form a crater with the dry ingredients, either on a clean surface or in a large bowl.

The wet ingredients (warm yeast, sugar water, and olive oil) will go in the middle of the crater.

It can be easier to use a fork at first to mix dry and wet, because you want to mix only a little at a time, starting with the edges.

If you want to use your hands, wash them first.

TA-DA!

When I'm still soft and gloopy, you can start forming gluten by pressing the dough out flat, then forming me into a ball a few times.

Forming and kneading can be very important for doughs that need gluten.

'OMPH!

Every time you squash or fold dough over, you make those nets of gluten align and strengthen.

This can create a chewy, crusty bread you can shape or mold however you like without using a pan or tin.

Soon I will gain strength, and you can shape me into a ball, and I'll stay that way.

Though I'm still feeling very mushy.

If the dough is still sticky, re-flour the surface **and** your hands.

This is when **real** kneading begins!

Press the heel of your hand into the dough, pushing about half of me out and forward.

Fold the section you pushed out back into the dough, folding me back up.

Give me a quarter turn to work with a new section next.

And press the next section out with the heel of your hand again.

Pressing me out...

...folding over...

...and turning...

...are done over and over.

This motion should be repeated fluidly and rhythmically.

It can be tiresome, but keep at it!

Agitate that gluten!

74

It's like I'm getting a **massage!**

Er! Except you're getting **tougher**, not more **relaxed!**

You're starting to feel like **leather**, not dough!

That's **great!** That's the gluten lining up!

How do you **know** when I'm *ready?*

When I pinch a piece of the dough, it will feel a bit like pinching an earlobe.

HE HE!

I'm all ears!

Also, when the dough is **poked...**

Ha ha!

POKE

Look what you did!

...it should *spring back* quickly.

Oh!

Put me in a large bowl lightly greased with oil, with cling wrap or a lid laid tightly across the top. Now it's time to proof*!

Proofing is when you let yeast grow undisturbed in specific conditions.

*Also called proving.

Proofing is done somewhere *warm,* but not **hot!**

Around 80°F is ideal. Too much warmer and yeast will multiply too quickly and drown.

Oh! The oven is still warm from the quick bread! Put me next to that!

If your oven is *off* and **cold,** put me on the middle rack...

place a bowl or pan of hot water under me on the lower rack...

then keep the door closed for an **hour.**

Give the yeast time to do its thing!

Then put me in the fridge!

The chilly fridge will make yeast multiply **slowly** but **evenly** through the dough.

So leave me in here for at least **four** hours or longer, like overnight.

76

Oh no! I forgot to take the dough out of the fridge, and let it warm up for an hour!

An hour?

Just kidding!

Korian took me out before you arrived!

I'm room temperature and ready to go!

HMPH!

CARELLA

Cut the dough in half so we can **each** make a pizza!

Flour a clean surface, and re-flour it anytime the dough starts to stick.

Lightly knead to redistribute the gas the yeast made overnight.

To make a classic round pizza shape, start by pressing it out with your fingers or using a rolling pin.

I'm gonna be a pizza!

If you're using a pre-heated pizza stone...

very carefully take the **hot** stone out of the oven with heat-safe gloves...

place on a safe surface like the oven burner...

and slide your pizza onto it.

SSSSSSSS

If you don't have a pizza stone, leave the pizza on the baking sheet...

and place the stone or sheet in the center of the oven and keep the door closed.

How long does pizza need to bake?

Till the dough is crispy and the toppings are hot.

Thinner dough like ours, about ten or fifteen minutes.

Thicker dough could take twenty to twenty-five minutes, or more.

15 minutes later...

My pizza on the baking sheet looks *fine,* but yours seems to be crispier, because of the pizza stone.

The pizza stone was so hot it started cooking the dough **before** it went into the oven.

I think the best way to explain is to make some—

CHEDDAR BISCUITS

Scones and biscuits are **almost** the same, except scones can have egg and are not fluffy or flaky.

And many people **expect** biscuits to be *savory*...

...and for scones to be *sweet*.

But that's **not** a set *rule*.

It's up to **you!**

Grate or chop the cheese and measure out the buttermilk.

Keep them in the fridge with the chopped butter.

Chop the parsley and set it aside.

Butter
1 stick

Buttermilk

Cheddar Cheese
1/2 cup

Parsley
1 TBSP

(chopped and cold)

1 cup
(cold)

(shredded and cold)

(chopped)

Preheat the oven to 475°F.

Leave your baking sheet **ungreased**.

The dry ingredients, including the spices, are all sifted together.

All-Purpose Flour	White Sugar	Baking Powder	Salt	Garlic Powder	Cayenne Pepper	Paprika
2 cups	2 tsp	1 TBSP	1 tsp	1 tsp	1/4 tsp	1/4 tsp

There are pieces of butter that remain large and mostly unmixed.

I will form the layers inside the dough when I bake and melt, leaving the air pockets behind.

Then there is flour and butter that's well mixed. This coats the flour in fat.

That way I can't absorb any liquid and uncoil my gluten.

There is also flour that's still dry and unmixed with any butter.

Flour that's dry will allow gluten to form as usual.

The amount of dry flour in the shaggy blend varies every time you make it.

When we add our liquid, the cold buttermilk, we don't add it all at once...

because we don't know how much dry unmixed flour there is to absorb it.

Adding more liquid to dry dough is better than adding more flour to wet dough...

since more flour means more gluten.

Add **all** the cheddar cheese in and **most** of the parsley in as well. Save a little for garnish.

89

90

No! Boo to shortening!

Butter is best!

Not true!

!

You again?

Many bakers **swear** by piecrusts made with shortening!

Shortening in crusts will still create layers **but** again, because it's nondiary, it won't have the flavor or rise of butter.

Tsk! There's more to piecrust than **flavor** and **rise!**

How about the times when you want to make intricate shapes and patterns?

Same as cutout cookies, an all-shortening crust won't spread, keeping the shape you want.

Butter's rise could puff and erase all your delicate work!

Sorry, I guess I like the **flavor** of a butter crust.

NOO!

Yeah!

You know, a pie isn't a pie without a filling!

A good time to make one is while the dough rests.

CLICK

Let's make apple! It's classic and easy!

First, we need six to eight medium-sized apples, peeled.

Remove the cores and cut into pieces or slices.

Mix the apple slices with seasoning, butter, and flour.

Flour will absorb the juices while the apples cook.

Keep the filling cold until ready to use.

White Sugar 1 cup

Flour 1/4 cup

Butter 2 TBSP (chopped and chilled)

Ground Nutmeg 1/4 tsp

Ground Cinnamon 1/2 tsp

Salt 1/2 tsp

Lemon Juice 2 TBSP

Let's talk in detail about the final steps in making the pie dough: our final roll and shaping into the pie plate.

If your crust is made well, rested, and everything is dusted with flour... I should roll out evenly, without cracking.

Rotate me occasionally while rolling. If I'm sticking to the surface, I need more flour on me.

wiggle

Roll me into a rectangle shape, a quarter-inch thick or thinner...

long enough to fit the pie plate across twice for a top and bottom crust.

Or you can divide me in two and roll me out one at a time, bottom crust first, then the top crust.

2 inches

Using the pie plate as a guide...

cut two circles out, about two inches larger than the diameter of the plate.

They don't have to be perfect.

What about pies that have a lattice crust or no top crust at all?

Some pie-crust designs are decorative, but certain fillings need specific crusts to bake right.

A double crust is made with dough, but crumb and cobbler crusts are sugar and flour or oats.

Many fruit pies need a top crust to act like a lid, steaming the fruit inside to cook fully.

A lattice crust isn't just for looks.

Most berry pies have a lattice-style crust to let steam escape, so the pie isn't soupy.

Single-crust pies, or tarts, have short baking times and often need to be blind-baked.

Blind baking is when the crust is baked either partway or fully before filling is added.

This is done when the crust and filling have different baking times or the filling is very wet.

Sage, look at all the baked goods you've made so far!

I'm really impressed with how hands-on you've become!

It's not as easy as **instant** baked goods...

but **now** I understand how it all works!

You were right...

a recipe **is** a kind of spell!

You've come a long way! But before you can say you understand the basics of baking, you need to tackle cake again.

I don't know. What about my pound cake?

Knowing how to make a basic cake from scratch is a **must**.

Most instant boxed cakes use *the Muffin Method...*

Traditional pound cakes use *the Creaming Method...*

But there is *another* method used for making cake!

The Egg Foam Method!

The Egg Foam Method makes a light, spongy cake, low in fat and easy to decorate.

Egg foam cakes use only whipped eggs to leaven and rise.

POP

To understand how a cake can rise using eggs **alone**, you need to learn a little more about **me**, the egg!

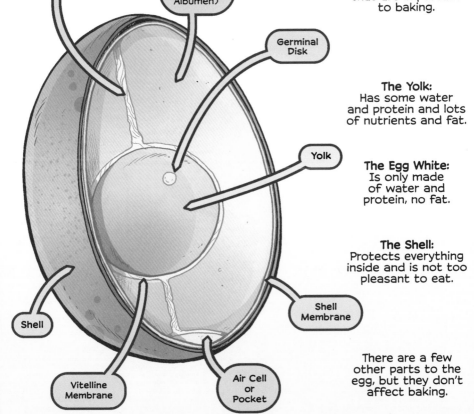

There are three main parts of the egg that are important to baking.

The Yolk:
Has some water and protein and lots of nutrients and fat.

The Egg White:
Is only made of water and protein, no fat.

The Shell:
Protects everything inside and is not too pleasant to eat.

There are a few other parts to the egg, but they don't affect baking.

Chalazae

Egg White (also called Albumen)

Germinal Disk

Yolk

Shell

Shell Membrane

Vitelline Membrane

Air Cell or Pocket

99

Egg white foams are described in recipes by their textures, as they are whipped more and more.

An electric mixer is the quickest way to make foam.

Whipping by hand is as effective but very time-consuming.

First, the egg whites get foamy. This stage is not an egg foam yet, but is when cream of tartar, the acid found in baking powder, can be added to help stabilize the proteins and grab more air as you keep going.

When the egg white foam gets thicker and keeps a smooth, loose shape when the whisk is removed, it's called a "soft peak." Sugar can be added now to make the foam stronger and shiny. Soft peak foam will add some rise to cake, but be sure to wait for stiff peaks!

Egg white foams that keep a firm shape when the whisk is removed are called "stiff peaks." A stiff peak egg foam should be strong enough to hold on to the bowl and not fall out when flipped upside down. This foam will add the most air and rise possible to an egg foam cake.

Whipping beyond stiff peak adds too much air and can cause the protein structure to collapse.

When there's too much air for the proteins to hold, their bonds with the air weaken and break, and the foam deflates.

SPONGE CAKE

Now that the eggs are separated, let's finish getting organized!

Since egg foams can deflate if they sit around, having everything you need out and ready to go will help you work quickly.

Oven preheated to 350°F

Flour and oil for greasing and dusting pans

Stand mixer with paddle and whisk attachments

9-inch round cake pans (2)

Sifter or fine sieve

A plain sponge cake is traditionally made with only eggs, flour, and sugar. We will add vanilla and salt for flavor and baking powder for an even rise.

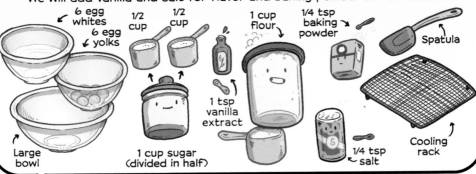

6 egg whites

6 egg yolks

1/2 cup

1/2 cup

1 cup flour

1/4 tsp baking powder

Spatula

1 tsp vanilla extract

Large bowl

1 cup sugar (divided in half)

1/4 tsp salt

Cooling rack

We whip the egg yolks first with the paddle. Add the vanilla and half the sugar as the paddle moves.

We know it's ready when the yolk is thick and sauce-like and falls off the paddle in a ribbon.

It sort of looks like thick yellow icing.

Put the thickened yolk aside in a large bowl and clean the stand mixer bowl and spatula.

Any yolk left in the stand mixer bowl could affect the whites.

Check!

Always whip the whites **after** the yolks so they don't sit around deflating.

And switch to the whisk attachment.

Whip the egg whites with the whisk attachment at medium-high speed.

WHIIIR

Stop the mixer periodically to check for soft peaks.

Add the other half of the sugar, slowly adding it to the whites as the whisk moves.

WHIR

There we go, stiff peaks!

We're ready to fold!

Add the other half of the egg white foam and fold it in the same way until **completely** incorporated.

We repeat the folding process next with flour instead of egg white foam.

When adding flour and other dry ingredients to an egg foam, you must *really sift*. No short-cuts with the whisk.

The egg foam fold only works with properly sifted flour. Unsifted flour will clump up.

Using the gentle fold to incorporate the sifted flour, I become a batter!

TADA!

Pour me evenly into two pans that have been greased and dusted with flour.

BLINK BLINK

Smooth out lumpy tops with a spatula.

But **don't shake** or **tap** us to smooth us out. It will shake out the air!

Get us into the oven right away!

Time wasted is time we're *deflating!*

15 minutes

Nice! The edges aren't stuck to the sides at all!

That's right!

I should come out of the pan easily.

That's how you know I'm *done!*

Let's frost you!

Not yet!

I must be room temperature or cooler to be frosted!

Frosting will *melt* off a **hot** cake!

Frosting made with butter and sugar is called *buttercream.*

Powdered sugar and butter is *American*-style buttercream.

French buttercream blends sugar, butter, and egg yolks.

Swiss-style buttercream, what we will make, uses egg whites.

4 egg whites

1/2 tsp salt

1 1/2 sticks butter at room temperature

Stand mixer

Whisk

1 cup sugar

1 tsp vanilla or other flavoring

Paddle and whisk attachments

This recipe requires a double boiler, which cooks using the steam of boiling water.

Water can only reach 212°F before turning to steam...

so whatever you place over that steam can't get any hotter than that and cooks slowly over lower heat.

Use a potholder. The bowl and the steam are hot. Whisk the ingredients constantly as they heat up, the sugar melts and the egg whites cook.

Sugar

Salt

Whisk

Egg Whites

Stand Mixer Bowl

I whisk the whole time?

Yes.

To check if the sugar and egg mixture is ready to take off the heat, dip a spoon into the bowl and allow it to cool until it's safe to touch...

...and rub the mixture between your fingers.

It feels grainy.

That means the sugar isn't melted yet, and it needs more time.

Here are the recipes Sage and Korian made in the book, in the order in which they appeared. You'll also find helpful baking tips, facts, and reminders.

The Baking Methods

Egg Foam Method
- Separate egg yolk & white as needed
- Whip separated egg
- Sift dry ingredients together
- Fold together as directed
- Bake

Biscuit Method
- Cut cold fat into dry ingredients
- Combine with liquid to create dough
- Rest
- Roll or shape
- Bake

Creaming Method
- Cream butter and white sugar
- Add eggs one at a time
- Add wet ingredients
- Add dry (or alternate wet/dry)
- Bake

Dough Method (with yeast)
- Bloom yeast if needed
- Combine dry ingredients with liquid and yeast
- Knead
- Rise (proof / punch / fold / rest)
- Shape (and score as needed)
- Bake

Muffin Method
- Sift dry ingredients together
- Mix wet ingredients together
- Combine wet and dry
- Bake

Bonus Method: Custard Method
- Uses tempering: Hot milk is added slowly to eggs, cooking them
- Is not a batter or dough
- Doesn't always require an oven

Classic Pound Cake
Makes one loaf or bundt cake.

Ingredients
- 1 cup butter
- 1 cup sugar
- 4 eggs
- 1 tsp vanilla extract
- 1/2 cup whole milk
- 2 cups flour
- 1 tsp baking powder
- 1/2 tsp salt

Special Tools
- Stand mixer with paddle attachment
- Wire cooling rack

Organize
1. Preheat oven to 350°F.
2. Grease and flour loaf pan or bundt pan.
3. Make sure butter is close to room temp, slightly soft.
4. Measure and sift together all dry ingredients: flour, baking powder, and salt.
5. Measure out and mix milk and vanilla.
6. Crack all eggs in a bowl together and whisk lightly.

Prepare
7. Put butter in stand mixing bowl with paddle attachment and beat on medium speed for 2 minutes.
8. Add sugar slowly and cream mixture together till fluffy.
9. Add eggs slowly, making sure they are fully incorporated.
10. Add vanilla extract.
11. Add about 1/3 of the dry ingredients and mix.
12. Add about 1/2 of the milk and mix until incorporated.
13. Repeat: 1/3 more dry, rest of milk, then rest of dry.
14. Make sure mixture is fully blended.

Bake
15. Pour into pan; smooth top with spoon but don't shake.
16. Bake 1 hour or until center is cooked.
17. Cool cake inside pan 15 minutes.
18. Carefully remove from pan and cool on wire rack.

Decorate with icing, fruit, honey, or powdered sugar.

What happens when cookies bake in the oven
Use your favorite cookie recipe and watch the magic happen.

92°F	+92°F	144°F	212°F	310°F	+360°F
Oven spring: Dough spreads, edges set.	Gases expand, steam rises and escapes.	Proteins and starch set to final shape.	Sugar liquefies from heat.	Maillard reaction: proteins brown.	Sugar caramelizes if oven is set hot enough.

Cooling solidifies sugar, and the dough deflates.

Effects of ingredients on cookies

Fat
- Butter: more tender
- Shortening: denser, chewier

Chemical Leavening
- Only baking soda: craggy top
- Only baking powder: smooth top

Eggs
- Extra egg white: taller, fluffy
- Extra egg yolk: fudgier, denser

Flour
- Less flour: crispier cookie
- More flour: doughy cookie
- Bread flour: chewy cookie
- Cake flour: softer cookie

Sugar
- All white sugar: thin and crispy
- All brown sugar: tall and moist

Replacing Sugar
To use honey, agave, or maple syrup instead of granulated sugar, follow a few simple steps.

Lower temperature (syrup burns faster)
Reduce temperature by 25°F.

Reduce liquid (syrup has more water)
For every 1 cup syrup, use 1/4 cup less liquid.

Add baking soda (needs extra lift)
For every 1 cup syrup, add 1/3 teaspoon.

Reduce sugar (syrup is sweeter)
For every 1 cup sugar, use 2/3 cup syrup.

Savory Corn Bread
Makes 9 muffins or one 9-inch pan.

Ingredients
- 1 cup flour
- 2 cups cornmeal
- 1/4 cup sugar
- 1 TBSP baking powder
- 1/2 tsp baking soda
- 1 tsp salt
- 1/2 cup melted butter
- 3 whole eggs
- 1 1/2 cups buttermilk
- 1/2 cup whole milk

Vegan
- 1 cup all-purpose flour
- 2 cups cornmeal
- 1/4 cup sugar
- 1 TBSP baking powder
- 1/2 tsp baking soda
- 1 tsp salt
- 1/2 cup oil
- 1/2 can creamed corn
- 2 cups milk alternative (unsweetend)
- 2 TBSP white vinegar

Organize
1. Preheat oven to 375°F.
2. Grease pan of your choice.
3. Butter and eggs to room temperature.

Prepare
4. Combine and whisk all dry ingredients: flour, cornmeal, baking powder, baking soda, and salt.
5. In a large bowl, combine and whisk all wet ingredients: sugar, melted butter, eggs, buttermilk, and whole milk.
6. Mix dry ingredients into wet ingredients and mix until incorporated.
7. Do not overmix; lumpy is good.

Bake
8. Pour batter into pan or muffin tray.
9. Bake for 20 to 30 minutes (test for doneness).
10. Cool for 15 minutes in pan before removing.

Best served warm and fresh.

Banana Bread
Makes one loaf.

Ingredients
- 1 stick butter, at room temperature
- 2/3 cup packed brown sugar
- 2–4 very ripe bananas (1 1/2 cups)
- 1/3 cup sour cream
- 2 eggs
- 1 1/2 cups flour
- 1 tsp salt
- 1 tsp baking soda
- 1/2 cup chopped walnuts (optional)

Special Tools
- Stand mixer with paddle attachment (if available)
- 9 x 5 inch loaf pan
- Wire cooling rack

Organize
1. Preheat oven to 350°F.
2. Grease the pan.
3. Combine eggs and sour cream.
4. Combine sugar, butter, and banana.
5. Combine and sift all dry ingredients (flour, baking soda, and salt).
6. Measure walnuts and set aside (optional).

Prepare
7. Cream butter, sugar, and banana using the paddle attachment for 2 minutes.
8. Add sour cream and eggs; mix thoroughly.
9. Add dry ingredients to wet ingredients, only mixing enough to incorporate while leaving lumps.
10. Gently stir in walnuts.

Bake
11. Pour in greased pan.
12. Bake about 60 minutes and test for doneness.
13. Cool in pan for 15 minutes.
14. Remove from pan and cool on rack.

Four ways to add yeast to your bread

Sourdough starter
A loose flour and water mix, which natural yeast will collect and grow on. Takes days.

Active dry yeast
Granulated dried yeast. Needs warm water to wake up or bloom from its dormant state.

Fresh yeast cake
Similar to a sourdough starter in texture, must be refrigerated, not widely available.

Instant yeast
Powdered dried yeast that will wake up immediately with moisture of any kind.

Bread techniques
Pizza dough is easy to make because it does not need to be perfect, but many breads are defined by careful shaping and scoring and by their crust.

Shape
- Shape affects the texture of the dough. Large, round loaves will have more soft bread inside; long, thin loaves have more crust.
- Shape is determined by factors like the type of flour used, how it's eaten, how it's cooked, and regional traditions.

Scoring
- Scoring is making cuts in the dough before it is baked. Most free-formed or nonpan loaves are scored.
- Gluten on the outside of the dough has more tension; the cuts break the outer gluten, permitting more oven spring while controlling the rise and shape while baking.

Crust
- Steaming bread with water while it's baking creates a thick crust. The water lowers the outer temperature of the bread, cooking it more slowly than the inside. This also hardens the starches that are cooking and drying on the surface.
- Sometimes glazes, like egg yolk or milk, are brushed on to create shine on crust.

Scoring, shaping, crusts, and glazes may also be used to identify the bread to both the baker and buyer visually, without having to ask or label them.

Pizza Crust (Part 1)
Makes one medium pizza crust or two personal sized.

Ingredients
- 1 cup warm water (90°F to 110°F)
- 1 tsp sugar
- 1 envelope dry **active** yeast (if using **instant** yeast, "blooming" is not neccesary)
- 2 TBSP olive oil
- 3 cups all-purpose flour
- 1 tsp salt

Special Tools
- Large mixing bowls (not metal)
- Cling wrap

Organize
1. Make sure all surfaces are dry and clean.
2. Mix and sift dry ingredients (flour and salt).
3. Mix warm water, sugar, oil, and yeast in a clean bowl and let it "bloom" for 10 minutes.
4. Use olive oil to grease a large bowl and set aside.

Prepare
5. Make a shallow "well" or crater with dry ingredients on the table or inside a bowl.
6. Pour the yeast water into the center.
7. Mix wet into dry using a fork, working around the edges of the well first.
8. Switch to using using your hands once most liquid is mixed in.
9. The dough should be smooth and slightly tacky, but not sticky and wet or dry and crumbly.
10. If very wet, add more flour (1–2 TBSP).
11. If very dry, add more water (1–2 TBSP).
12. Knead the dough for about 10 minutes.
13. Form the dough into a smooth ball and place in the large oiled bowl.
14. Cover bowl tightly with cling wrap and place in a warm area to proof (around 80°F is ideal).
15. Leave for 1 hour; should double in size.
16. Refrigerate for 4 hours or overnight.

Pizza Crust (Part 2)

Ingredients
- All-purpose flour (as needed)
- Semolina flour (as needed)

Special Tools
- Cookie sheet
- Pizza stone if available
- Cast-iron cookware if available inside oven

Organize
1. Take dough out of fridge at least an hour before use to warm up.
2. Preheat your oven to 475°F.
3. Preheat pizza stone in oven if using.
4. Keep dough whole for one pizza or cut dough in half for two smaller pizzas.

Prepare
5. Flour your work surface and knead dough for 2 minutes.
6. Press with fingers or roll out to a round shape half the size of your final pizza.
7. If it's very stretchy and won't stay shaped, cover with cling wrap and let rest 10 minutes.
8. Hold part of the dough up by gently placing fingers underneath the edge and carefully stretching it up and out, section by section.
9. Dust a cookie sheet with semolina and place dough on top.
10. Add toppings of your choice (sauce, cheese, etc).

Bake
11. If using a pizza stone, carefully take out (it will be extremely hot) and slide the pizza onto it from the cookie sheet; return to oven right away.
12. If no pizza stone available, put the cookie sheet with the pizza on it directly into the oven.
13. If the pizza is thin, bake for 10–15 minutes.
14. Bake thicker crusts with more toppings 20-25 minutes.
15. When finished, let it cool a few minutes, but serve warm.

Cheddar Biscuits

Makes 5 to 7 biscuits.

Ingredients
- 2 cups all-purpose flour
- 2 tsp sugar
- 1 TBSP baking powder
- 1 tsp salt
- 1 tsp garlic powder
- 1/4 tsp cayenne
- 1/4 tsp paprika
- 1 stick butter, cold (plus extra to melt)
- 1 cup buttermilk
- 1/2 cup shredded cheddar cheese
- 1 TBSP fresh chopped parsley

Special Tools
- Baking sheet
- Wire cooling rack
- Rolling pin
- Round cookie cutter

Organize
1. Preheat oven to 475°F.
2. Measure buttermilk and cheese out, then keep cold.
3. Chop cold butter into uneaven pea-size (or smaller) pieces and then keep cold.

Prepare
4. Combine and sift all dry ingredients in a large bowl, spices included.
5. "Cut" cold butter into dry with fingers or pastry blender till "shaggy" texture.
6. Add cheddar cheese, half the parsley, and 3/4 of the buttermilk to the shaggy mixture. (Add the rest of the buttermilk if it seems too dry.)
7. Use a spatula to combine, folding the wet batter onto itself; finish with hands if desired.
8. For best results, cover dough with cling wrap and rest in fridge for 30 minutes.
9. Flour surface and rolling pin well.
10. Roll out with rolling pin on clean surface.
11. Fold dough over in thirds.
12. Lightly roll again, 3/4- to 1-inch thickness.
13. Cut out square shapes with a knife or use a circle-shaped cutter, about 2 1/2" diameter.

Bake
14. Transfer to baking sheet, keeping them close together.
15. Bake 10–15 minutes.
16. Let cool on baking sheet for 2 minutes.
17. Brush with melted butter and sprinkle with parsley (optional).
18. Serve warm or transfer to cooling rack.

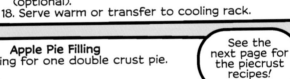

Apple Pie Filling

Makes filling for one double crust pie.

See the next page for the piecrust recipes!

Ingredients
- Double crust pie dough
- 1/4 cup all-purpose flour
- 1 cup white sugar
- 1/2 tsp cinnamon
- 1/2 tsp salt
- 1/4 tsp ground nutmeg
- 2 TBSP lemon juice
- 2 TBSP butter, chilled and cubed
- 6 large or 8 medium-sized apples

Organize
1. Preheat oven to 475°F.
2. Keep dough cold while making filling.
3. Peel, core, and slice apples.
4. Mix flour, sugar, spices, and salt.
5. Mix apples, lemon juice, and butter.

Prepare
6. Combine the flour mixture into the apple mixture in batches, so the apples are evenly coated.
7. Get pie dough ready for filling.
8. Place apples inside the dough and pie plate in a domed shape.
9. Cover with top dough and seal the crusts together.
10. Make a few steam vents on the top.
11. Brush crust with beaten egg and sprinkle with white sugar (optional).

Bake
12. Bake at 475°F for 15 minutes.
13. Lower temperature to 350°F; continue to bake for 30–45 more minutes till golden.
14. Only open oven if edges are cooking fast, to cover them with tinfoil to prevent burning.
15. Let cool for an hour before serving.

Double Piecrust
Makes one double crust pie.

Ingredients

Crust
- 2 1/2 cups all-purpose flour
- 1 tsp salt
- 2 sticks cold butter
- 1/2 cup cold water

Filling of your choice

Special Tools
- Rolling pin

Organize
1. Rough chop cold butter into uneaven pea-size (or smaller) pieces; keep cold.
2. Measure water and keep cold.
3. Combine and sift dry ingredients (flour and salt).
4. Oven temperature will depend on the filling; check with your recipe.
5. Have the filling of your choice prepared and ready.

Prepare
6. "Cut" butter into dry ingredients with fingers or pastry blender till "shaggy."
7. Add half the water to butter/flour mixture.
8. Use a spatula or hands to incorporate ingredients, folding it onto itself and making sure all water is absorbed.
9. If it's very dry, add more water. If it's too wet, add more flour.
10. Cover with cling wrap and rest in fridge for at least one hour.
11. Flour surface and rolling pin well.
12. Roll dough thin, fold over in thirds, and repeat till rolled larger than two pie plates (for top and bottom).
13. Cut two circles of dough out at least 2 inches larger in diameter than the pie plate being used.
14. Lay the bottom crust into the pie plate and gently press it in.
15. Fill with filling of your choice.
16. Cover with top crust and seal edges by using fingers to pinch together or by pressing with a fork.

Bake
17. Egg wash or crust decoration is optional.
18. Oven temperature and time will depend on the filling; bake according to your recipe and filling.

Single Piecrust
Makes one single-crust pie or tart.

Ingredients
- the same as double crust recipe, but cut amounts in half
- add 2 tsp of sugar for sweeter crust (optional)

Special Tools
- Pie weights or dry beans
- Parchment paper

Organize
1. Preheat oven to 350°F.
2. Same organizing as a double crust.

Prepare
3. Prepare crust the same as double crust, but only cut out one circle.
4. The crust must be laid into the pie plate and cut, shaped, or crimped exactly as you want the finished product to look.

Bake
5. Lay parchment paper into your shaped dough.
6. Fill evenly with pie weights or dry beans.
7. Bake 15–20 minutes; you want a little color, but not a full bake.
8. Let cool before filling and baking again according to the filling recipe.

Simple Sponge Cake
Makes one two-tiered cake.

Organize
1. Combine and sift dry ingredients.
2. Preheat oven to 350°F.
3. Separate eggs into whites and yolks.
4. Grease and dust two 9-inch round cake pans.

Ingredients
- 6 eggs, room temperature
- 1 cup white sugar, divided in half
- 1 tsp vanilla extract
- 1 cup flour
- 1/4 tsp baking powder
- 1/4 tsp salt

Special Tools
- Stand mixer with both paddle and whisk attachments
- 9-inch round cake pans (1 or 2)
- Wire cooling rack
- Sifter or fine mesh strainer

Prepare
5. Put 6 yolks in stand mixer bowl and use paddle attachment at medium-high speed.
6. Slowly pour in half the white sugar (1/2 cup) and vanilla as you beat.
7. Continue to beat until the yolk lightens in color, and when the paddle is removed, a thick "ribbon" of yolk should fall off of it.
8. Transfer yolk mixture to a large clean bowl.
9. Thoroughly clean all tools used, so no yolk remains.
10. Add 6 egg whites to clean stand mixer bowl.
11. Use whisk attachment at medium-high speed and watch for a light foam or froth to start to form.
12. Slowly add the other half of the sugar while continuing to whisk.
13. Once stiff peaks appear, take half the egg white foam and fold into yolk mixture.
14. When mostly combined, fold in the rest of egg white foam.
15. Sift the dry ingredients into the egg mixture and fold in till fully incorporated and batter forms.

Bake
17. Divide the batter evenly between the cake pans.
18. Smooth batter if needed but don't tap or shake.
19. Bake for 15-20 minutes.
20. If baking unevenly, rotate inside oven halfway through.
21. When fully cooked, the edges should come away from the pan.
22. Let rest in pan for 5 minutes, then invert onto wire rack to cool completely.

Swiss Meringue Buttercream
Makes enough frosting for one cake.

Ingredients
- 4 egg whites
- 1 cup white sugar
- 1/2 tsp salt
- 1 1/2 sticks butter at room temperature
- 1 tsp vanilla or other flavoring

Special tools
- Stand mixer with both paddle and whisk attachments
- Thermometer if available
- Pot for double boiler
- Regular whisk

Organize
1. Separate eggs and discard yolks or use in other recipes.
2. Cut butter into tablespoons.
3. Fill pot halfway with water and bring to a boil on stove.

Prepare
4. Put egg whites, sugar, and salt in stand mixer bowl, and put on top of boiling water to create a double boiler.
5. Whisk constantly as the sugar heats up and melts, cooking the egg whites.
6. Make sure it doesn't go over 180°F, or feel with your fingers for graininess of unmelted sugar.
7. When 170°F–180°F and sugar is completely melted, transfer to stand mixer.
8. Whip on medium speed with whisk attachment, till bowl is cool to the touch and very stiff peaks can form.
9. Switch whisk attachment for paddle.
10. Add butter (a tablespoon at a time) and vanilla extract while paddle moves.
11. Leave in bowl or fill piping bag.
12. Chill in fridge for 15 minutes before use.

Lemon Meringue Pie

Combine methods with this bonus recipe using a blind-baked crust, custard filling, and egg foam topping.

Ingredients

Single piecrust, blind-baked and cooled

Lemon Filling
- 1 1/4 cup sugar
- 1/3 cup cornstarch
- 1/4 tsp salt
- 1 1/2 cups milk
- 2 TBSP butter at room temperature
- 4 egg yolks
- 1/2 cup lemon juice
- 1 TBSP lemon zest

Meringue Topping
- 4 egg whites
- 6 TBSP sugar
- 1/4 tsp cream of tartar
- 1/2 tsp vanilla

Special Tools
- Hand or stand mixer with whisk

Organize
1. Oven preheated to 375°F.
2. Egg yolks and whites separated and in large bowls.

Prepare

Lemon Filling
3. Combine sugar, cornstarch, salt, and milk in heavy pot over medium heat.
4. Whisk constantly until it starts to steam.
5. Pour half of hot milk mixture slowly into the egg yolks while whisking.
6. Slowly pour the egg and milk mixture into the remaining hot milk over heat while whisking.
7. Continue to whisk and cook until the mixture becomes a thick pudding consistency.
8. Remove from the heat and add lemon juice, lemon zest, and butter, whisking until combined.
9. Pour the filling into the cooled blind-baked piecrust.

Meringue Topping
10. Beat egg whites till foamy.
11. Add cream of tartar and vanilla and continue to beat.
12. Add sugar slowly while continuing to beat.
13. Beat till shiny, smooth, stiff peaks form.

Bake
14. Top lemon filling with meringue.
15. Bake 5-10 minutes till the meringue turns golden brown on the edges.

Continued Reading

How Baking Works: Exploring the Fundamentals of Baking Science
Paula Figoni (John Wiley & Sons, 2010)
A chemistry-based analysis of baking and recipes, including the science of baking without sugar or gluten.

The Baking Bible
Rose Levy Beranbaum (Houghton Mifflin Harcourt, 2014)
A beautiful and slightly more advanced cookbook, with clear, straightforward ingredient lists and instructions.

The Dessert Bible: The Best of American Home Cooking
Christopher Kimball (Little, Brown and Company, 2015)
Hundreds of recipes with clearly described techniques and an analysis of what tools and tips work best in practical use.

I'm Just Here for More Food: Food x Mixing + Heat = Baking
Alton Brown (Stewart, Tabori & Chang, 2004)
A clear analysis of baking from a scientific viewpoint, in both its approach to ingredients and the techniques used.

Conversions and Measurements

Abbreviations	
°F	degrees Fahrenheit
°C	degrees Celsius
fl oz	fluid ounce
oz	ounce
tsp	teaspoon
TBSP	tablespoon
g	gram
lb	pound
pt	pint
qt	quart
gal	gallon
ml	milliliter

Fahrenheit to Celsius
275°F · 140°C
300°F · 150°C
325°F · 165°C
350°F · 180°C
375°F · 190°C
400°F · 200°C
425°F · 220°C
450°F · 230°C
475°F · 240°C

Weight Conversions
1 oz · 28 g
1 lb · 454 g

Dry Measurements	
1/16 tsp	"A pinch"
1/8 tsp	"A dash"
3 tsp	1 TBSP
1/8 cup	2 TBSP
1/4 cup	4 TBSP
1/3 cup	5 TBSP + 1 tsp
1/2 cup	8 TBSP
3/4 cup	12 TBSP
1 cup	16 TBSP
1 lb	16 oz

Liquid Measurements		
8 fl oz	1 cup	
1 pt	2 cup	16 fl oz
1 qt	2 pt	4 cup
1 gal	4 qt	16 cup

US and Metric Conversions		
1/5 tsp		1 ml
1 tsp		5 ml
1 TBSP		15 ml
1 fl oz		30 ml
1/5 cup		50 ml
1 cup		240 ml
2 cup	1 pt	470 ml
4 cup	1 qt	.95 liter
4 qt	1 gal	3.8 liters

Butter				
1 TBSP	14 g			
1 stick	4 oz	113 g	8 TBSP	1/2 cup
4 stick	16 oz	452 g	32 TBSP	2 cups

Lemons & Limes (Approximate)		
1 lemon	1–3 TBSP juice	1 TBSP zest
4 lemon	1/2 cup juice	1/4 cup zest

Chocolate		
1 oz	1/4 cup grated	40 g
6 oz chips	1 cup	160 g
1 cup powder	115 g	

First Second

Copyright © 2019 by Falynn Koch

Published by First Second
First Second is an imprint of Roaring Brook Press,
a division of Holtzbrinck Publishing Holdings Limited Partnership
175 Fifth Avenue, New York, NY 10010
All rights reserved

Library of Congress Control Number: 2018938072

Paperback ISBN: 978-1-250-15006-6
Hardcover ISBN: 978-1-250-15005-9

Our books may be purchased in bulk for promotional, educational, or business use.
Please contact your local bookseller or the Macmillan Corporate and Premium Sales Department
at (800) 221-7945 ext. 5442 or by e-mail at MacmillanSpecialMarkets@macmillan.com.

First edition, 2019
Edited by Robyn Chapman and Bethany Bryan
Expert consultant: Kelly Vass
Book design by Rob Steen

Printed in China by 1010 Printing International Limited, North Point, Hong Kong

Penciled, inked, and colored in Photoshop with Kyle Webster digital brushes Drawing Box:
Non Photo Blue Pro and Inkbox: Pocket Brush 1 along with a variety of other Photoshop brushes.

Paperback: 10 9 8 7 6 5 4 3 2 1
Hardcover: 10 9 8 7 6 5 4 3 2 1